Jazzin' Americana

FOR TWO

5 Late Elementary to Early Intermediate Piano Duets That Celebrate American Jazz

Wynn-Anne Rossi

Welcome to *Jazzin' Americana for Two*. This unique series is a journey through the jazz genre, honoring the history, diverse styles, and fabulous musicians who made this music great. While delving into appealing jazz styles, the performers will become familiar with the names of famous musicians like Mary Lou Williams, Charlie Parker, and Duke Ellington. From blues and bebop to boogie and rock, American jazz has made its profound mark on the music of the world.

Each duet is enhanced by interesting facts to awaken curiosity and broaden music education. Please encourage additional jazz listening and research as students navigate through the different styles. Rhythm workshops are included to help students count, then "feel" tricky jazz rhythms.

Please note that improvisation is not the focus of this series. Though improvisation is a key element in jazz, these books are designed as an introduction to the sounds of jazz. However, teachers and students may find it energizing to use a certain jazz style, left-hand pattern, or chord sequence as a springboard for free experimentation.

Enjoy this heartfelt, historic journey through *Jazzin' Americana for Two*!

Wynn-Anne Rossi

Contents

Alfred Music
P.O. Box 10003
Van Nuys, CA 91410-0003
alfred.com

Copyright © 2018 by Alfred Music
All rights reserved. Printed in USA.

ISBN-10: 1-4706-3982-3
ISBN-13: 978-1-4706-3982-2
Cover Illustration
Instrument Icons: © gettyimages.com / Leontura

Pioneer Rag

Benjamin Robertson "Ben" Harney
(1872–1938) was a pioneer of ragtime
music. His "You've Been a Good Old
Wagon but You Done Broke Down,"
written in 1895, is one of the earliest
ragtime compositions on record.

Rhythm Workshop

Tap rhythm 3x daily.

mm. 9–10

Secondo

Wynn-Anne Rossi

Rhythm Workshop

Tap rhythm 3x daily.

mm. 7–8

Pioneer Rag

Benjamin Robertson "Ben" Harney (1872–1938) was a pioneer of ragtime music. His "You've Been a Good Old Wagon but You Done Broke Down," written in 1895, is one of the earliest ragtime compositions on record.

Primo

Wynn-Anne Rossi

Playfully, steady ($\quad$ = 120)

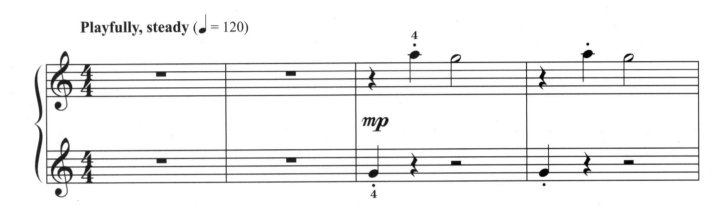

Royal Blue for Mary Lou

Mary Lou Williams (1910–1981) was a prominent jazz pianist and prolific composer. She produced over 100 records and was a mentor to several famous jazz musicians, including pianist Thelonious Monk (1917–1982) and trumpeter Miles Davis (1926–1991).

Rhythm Workshop

Tap rhythm 3x daily.

Secondo

Wynn-Anne Rossi

Rhythm Workshop

Tap rhythm 3x daily.

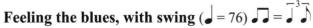

Royal Blue for Mary Lou

Mary Lou Williams (1910–1981) was a prominent jazz pianist and prolific composer. She produced over 100 records and was a mentor to several famous jazz musicians, including pianist Thelonious Monk (1917–1982) and trumpeter Miles Davis (1926–1991).

Primo

Wynn-Anne Rossi

Feeling the blues, with swing ($\quarter = 76$)

Secondo

Welcome to the Savoy

The Savoy Ballroom opened its doors on March 12, 1926, in the heart of Harlem, New York City. It was the home of famous big band competitions, and all people were welcome—as long as you could dance!

Secondo

Wynn-Anne Rossi

Rhythm Workshop

Tap rhythm 3x daily.

Welcome to the Savoy

The Savoy Ballroom opened its doors on March 12, 1926, in the heart of Harlem, New York City. It was the home of famous big band competitions, and all people were welcome—as long as you could dance!

Primo

Wynn-Anne Rossi

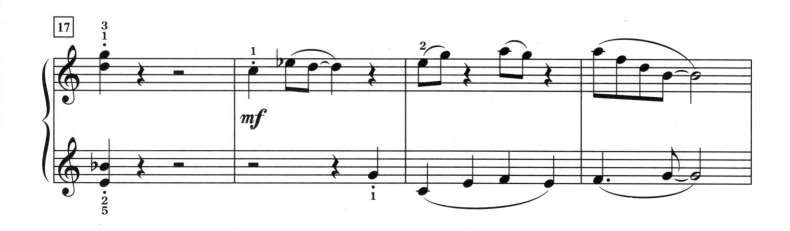

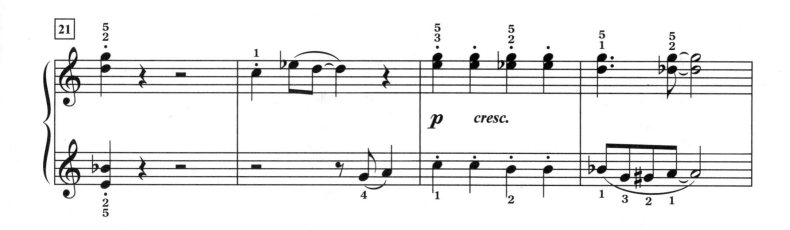

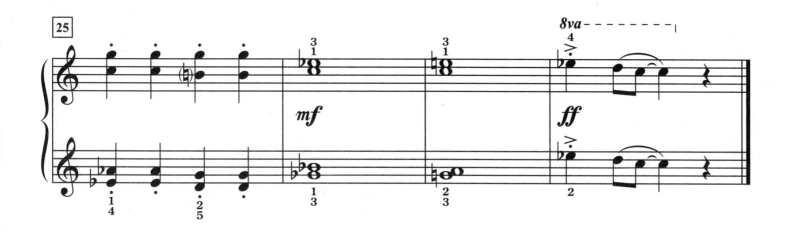

Crazy Chops

"Chops" is slang for a musician's technical abilities, including speed. Maxwell "Max" Roach (1924–2007) was a famous jazz percussionist with awesome chops. He often performed with legendary saxophonist Charlie Parker (1920–1955) and composer and bandleader Duke Ellington (1899–1974).

Rhythm Workshop

Tap rhythm 3x daily.

mm. 1–2

Secondo

Wynn-Anne Rossi

Crazy fast! (♩ = 138)

mp

(even eighths)

mf

Rhythm Workshop

Tap rhythm 3x daily.

mm. 2–3

Crazy Chops

"Chops" is slang for a musician's technical abilities, including speed. Maxwell "Max" Roach (1924–2007) was a famous jazz percussionist with awesome chops. He often performed with legendary saxophonist Charlie Parker (1920–1955) and composer and bandleader Duke Ellington (1899–1974).

Primo

Wynn-Anne Rossi

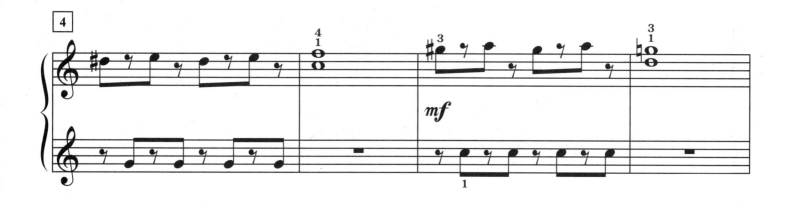

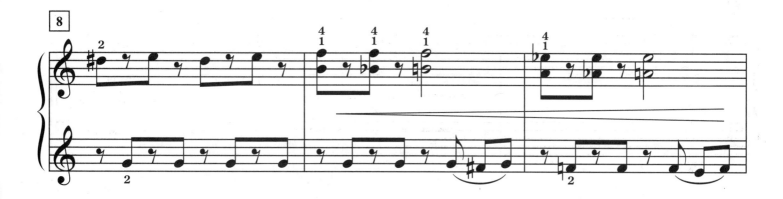

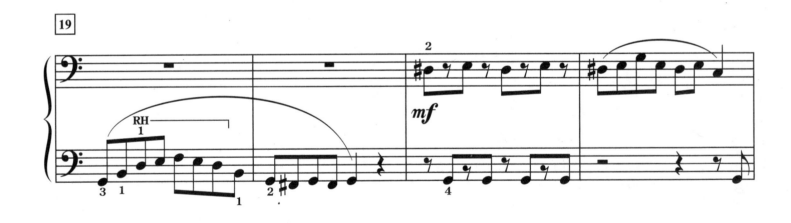

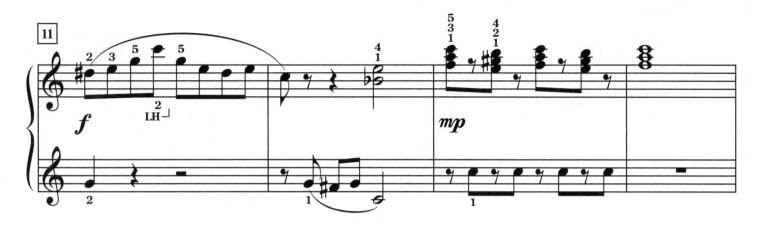

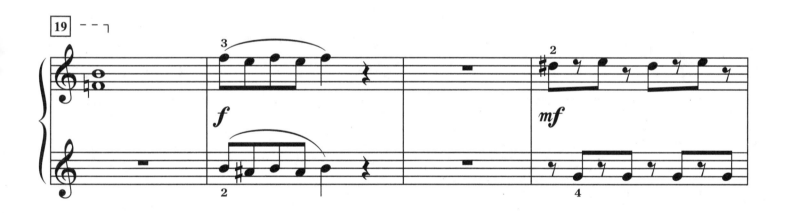

Hancock Rock

Headhunters, recorded in 1973 by pianist/composer Herbert "Herbie" Hancock (b. 1940), was the fastest-selling jazz album of all time. It explored *jazz-rock*, a new genre of jazz, which mixed great grooves with heavy bass and captured the attention of new audiences.

Rhythm Workshop

Tap rhythm 3x daily.

mm. 1–2

Secondo

Wynn-Anne Rossi

With a heavy beat (♩ = 112)

Hancock Rock

Rhythm Workshop

Tap rhythm 3x daily.

mm. 5–6

Headhunters, recorded in 1973 by pianist/composer Herbert "Herbie" Hancock (b. 1940), was the fastest-selling jazz album of all time. It explored *jazz-rock*, a new genre of jazz, which mixed great grooves with heavy bass and captured the attention of new audiences.

Primo

Wynn-Anne Rossi

With a heavy beat (♩ = 112)

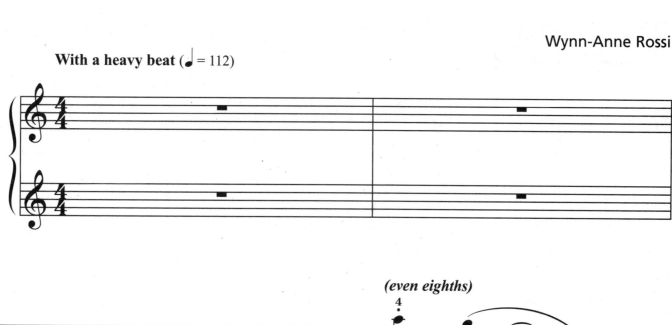

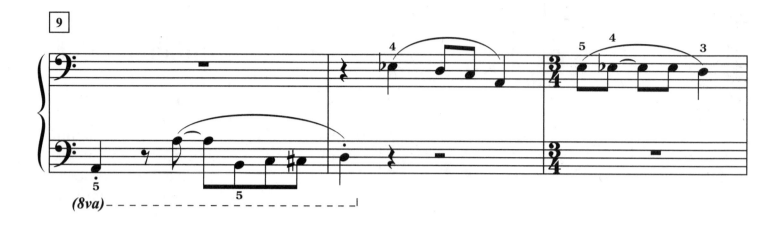

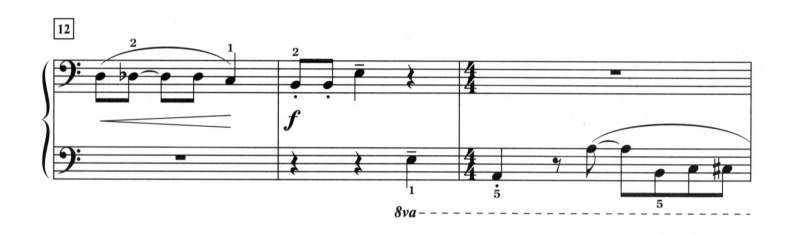

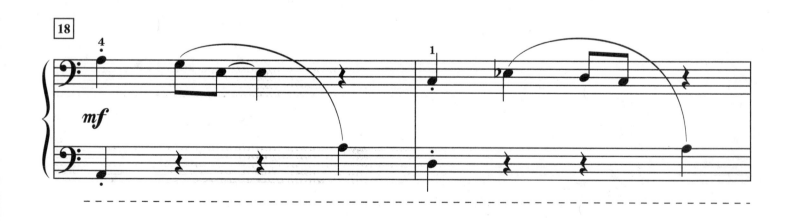

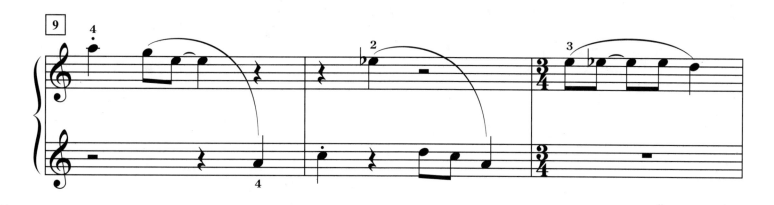

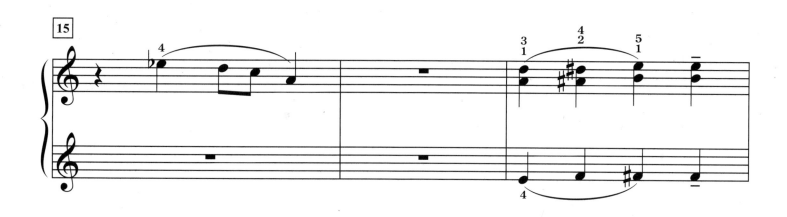

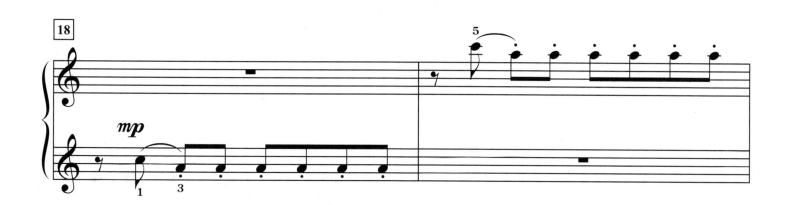

Secondo

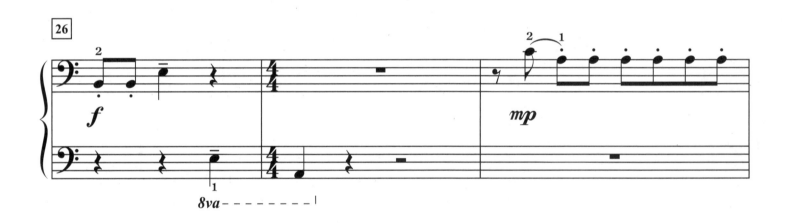

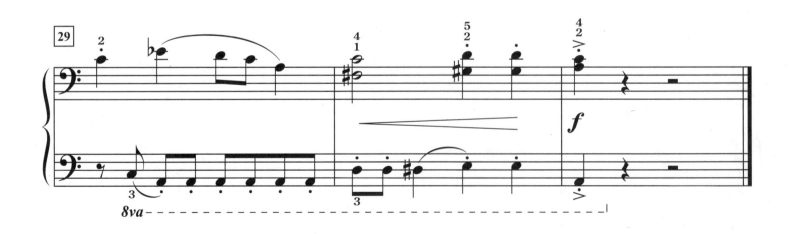

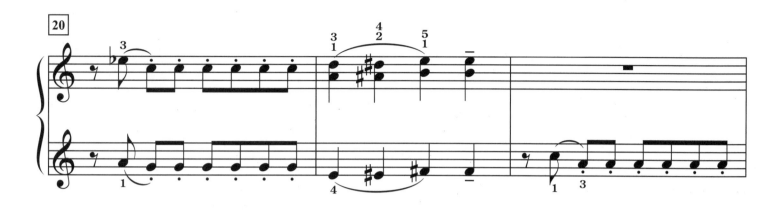

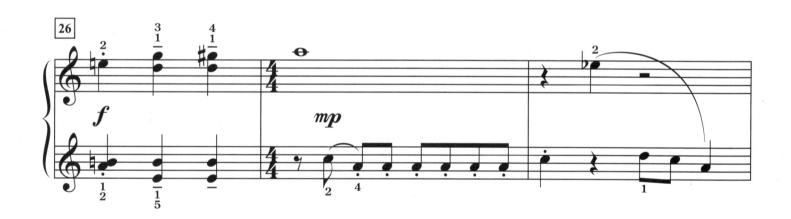

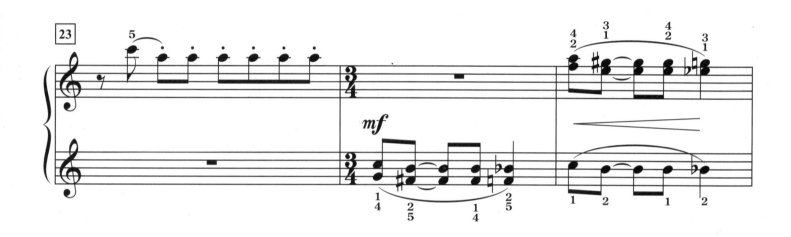

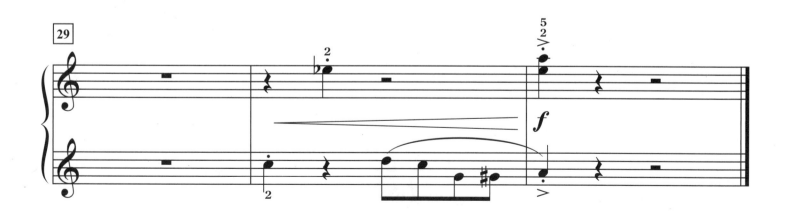